AF808080

From the author of

What My Mom Taught Me About Money

Mom's Money Lessons

Making Sense out of Your Dollars

By

Teneshia LaFaye

INFINITY PUBLISHING

All rights reserved. No part of this book shall be reproduced or transmitted in any form or by any means, electronic, mechanical, magnetic, photographic including photocopying, recording or by any information storage and retrieval system, without prior written permission of the publisher. No patent liability is assumed with respect to the use of the information contained herein. Although every precaution has been taken in the preparation of this book, the publisher and author assume no responsibility for errors or omissions. Neither is any liability assumed for damages resulting from the use of the information contained herein.

Copyright © 2012 by Teneshia LaFaye
Front cover photo courtesy of iStockphoto
Back cover photo taken by Jennifer Harvey

ISBN 978-0-7414-7656-2 Paperback
ISBN 978-0-7414-7657-9 eBook
Library of Congress Control Number: 2012939368

Printed in the United States of America

Published January 2013

INFINITY PUBLISHING
1094 New DeHaven Street, Suite 100
West Conshohocken, PA 19428-2713
Toll-free (877) BUY BOOK
Local Phone (610) 941-9999
Fax (610) 941-9959
Info@buybooksontheweb.com
www.buybooksontheweb.com

Foreword

By Darian Demetri, a college student and Teneshia's son

I'm the kind of person who always has his mind made up, even before someone starts to tell me about something. When my mom talks to me about finances, it usually goes in one ear and out the other. For me the best teacher is experience. I don't have to listen to her lecture me about money because I've experienced the bad things she has done with money and told myself to never do those things. However, reading this book has taught me some fundamental principles without having to listen to my mom lecture me, which no young adult wants to hear.

After days of resisting, I finally agreed to read her book. Surprisingly, it highlighted the things I do wrong and some that I do right. From basic things that are discussed in this book, such as getting a job you enjoy or not spending your entire paycheck. To critical things that young adults should know, such as her 60-20-10-10© rule for budgeting money as well as establishing credit.

My favorite part of the book is the chapter on treating yourself, which is something I do very often. During my first semester in college, the very first thing I bought with my financial aid refund check was a $200 Fossil watch that I always wanted. By doing so, I treated myself, spending less than 10% of the $2,500 I had remaining from financial aid. And whenever I wear that watch, I feel happy and accomplished, knowing I could afford it because, as my mom says, never spend more than 10% of your savings to treat yourself. She also says you should give yourself a regular allowance of 10% of your paycheck.

In her book, my mom explains how to create a budget, which I need because I manage the finances for a fashion photo rating site, www.Faddest.com, that I created with one of my best friends. We have a set budget for marketing and for improvements to the website. This is an example of me having a job that I love, as my mom recommends in her book. Faddest is something I would work at 12 hours a day with no pay. I also get paid selling life insurance to follow in my mom's footsteps, which allows me to have money to buy the latest fashion.

I didn't always have it so good. My best friends can tell you that in elementary school I used to wear faded high water pants and the same black Target brand shoes to school every day. And at the time, I had never been out-of-town, not even to Orlando, which is just 90 minutes up the road, because my parents made a lot of mistakes with money and that falls back on their parents who made mistakes with money.

Even though my parents were college graduates making a combined $70,000 per year, they were always broke. Too broke to buy me new clothes. Too broke to go on a vacation. Too broke to buy me one of those electric Fisher Price cars that I always wanted.

My mom says it's too bad there's no high school class to really teach you about money because she really failed at spending it wisely, and I know many other adults that are doing the same. Some of my friends' parents have already lost their homes.

Now we have a newly-built house in a desirable area of town and I can afford to shop, put gas in my SUV, and most importantly save. It's all about knowing how to use money.

I want to continue to live well when I move out from my mom's house, so I am heeding her advice about money.

My mom was born to a talented, young hair stylist and a medical surgeon. Her parents never married, and her stepdad helped to raise her.

My grandmother was a very successful hairstylist, so my mom was raised in a very nice house in one of the wealthiest areas in town, like where we live now.

My mom's classmates thought she was rich because she always had new clothes, new shoes, and well-groomed hair. Her parents took her to Red Lobster as regularly as a trip to McDonald's. And every summer, her parents took her to a huge Fashion Show in Atlanta, and they once took her to the World's Fair, the biggest fair on the planet, in New Orleans.

My mom didn't consider herself rich. She didn't love money. Unlike me, she hated when her parents took her shopping every other week.

But my mom learned of the importance of money when her parents divorced while she was in middle school. Life wasn't so rosy when her regular shopping trips quickly turned into yearly shopping trips. The vacations stopped, but they were able to keep their nice house and my mom's grandfather financed a brand new car for my mom in high school.

My mom was determined to go to college and get a high-paying job to be able to afford her former lifestyle.

Now, she has regained that lifestyle, but it didn't happen as soon as she had originally planned.

It took her more than 10 years after she graduated from college to achieve financial success.

It shouldn't have taken that long because she had no student loans. She attended college on federal grants and scholarships. She already had her first couple of paychecks, a month before receiving her journalism degree, because she was hired to work at a newspaper in Tallahassee before her college graduation ceremony.

She returned to her hometown in Jacksonville and became an award-winning sports writer, traveling to write stories about the likes of Tiger Woods, Michael Jordan, LeBron James, Cal Ripken and hometown hero Bob Hayes.

She was 24, making $40,000 a year and driving an Acura TL. My mom was admired in the community; considered a celebrity by my classmates and she appeared to be living life in the fast lane.

But except for myself and close relatives, no one had any idea of my mom's personal struggles with money. I was late to school one morning because my mom's car was repossessed overnight.

All the while, my mom was making good money and was a locally-famous sports writer. Yet we had no money to do anything.

You're probably wondering what this has to do with you. Well when you're growing up, you think you're going to get a high-paying job, buy a lot of clothes, drive a nice car and vacation around the world. But many people aren't living those lifestyles because they never learned how to handle money. Just look at your parents and other relatives.

My mom didn't know how to handle money, so she didn't live on a budget. And she spent more money than she made. So even though she made $40,000 a year, she had to go to cash advance stores and pawn shops for additional money to pay her bills. Every pay period, she spent her entire paycheck to pay off cash advance centers and pawn shops. My dad was in the same situation, and he has a master's degree. The financial burden became so overwhelming that my parents and I had to move in with relatives.

Can you imagine graduating from college, living on your own making a combined $70,000 a year, being a success in your career and having to move back in with your parents?

That's what my mom and dad had to do, and actually a lot of adults are doing that now while the U.S. recovers from the Great Recession of 2008. Many people are barely making ends meet. It just goes to show you that we are all missing out on a good financial education.

My mom overcame her financial ignorance by reading books about money and learning how to use it wisely. Hopefully, you will read her book and avoid what my mom went through or overcome your bad financial habits like she did. She has taught me financial principles that will allow me to keep up my superficial lifestyle, albeit on a budget, when I graduate from college.

Acknowledgements

This book is my second and has been on my heart for the last two years. But between work appointments and raising a family, I never could find time to write this book until meeting with online marketing rep Ron MacNeil. He was supposed to be selling me a service to put my financial advice blog, www.mytensense.com, at the top of Google's search engine. Instead, he spent our meeting encouraging me to finish my book by picking a day out of each week for "Teneshia" time to focus on writing my book. I procrastinated for a few weeks and finally decided to allocate time for writing on Fridays. Three months later, I finished my book and I am very appreciative to Ron for encouraging me to make time in my busy schedule to write this book that I feel is critical for the financial well-being of so many.

I also am very thankful to Kemal Gasper, a bank branch manager, and financial advisor Bob Horne for verifying my accuracy on several financial topics.

I especially would like to thank my two sons, Darian Jr. and Dominick. They are the most precious people in my life and the reason I work so hard. I appreciate the patience of my youngest son Dominick, who often had to wait to go outside to play catch with me while I worked on my book. Darian inspired me to step out and write a book when he wrote a book explaining HTML coding for kids at the age of 10. He also has written a couple of 40,000-plus word young adult fiction books that haven't been published yet. I appreciate Darian finally taking time out of his busy schedule as a full-time college student, student ambassador, class officer, insurance agent and fashion web site creator to read the final draft of my book and endorse it by writing a Foreword on why people should read my book.

I also would like to thank my mother and grandfather. My mother has always encouraged and supported me in everything I've done, and she prayed for my strength during a very depressing time in my life that I have since overcome. My grandfather has bailed me out of so many financial jams and has been a father figure to me by encouraging me to believe in myself and providing for my needs and many wants.

Finally, I would like to thank my Lord, the Father, the Son Jesus and the Holy Spirit for blessing me with the talent to be a good writer and editor and for giving me the assignment of teaching the masses financial responsibility. I also appreciate the desire and tenacity that has been ingrained in me by my Creator.

Table of Contents

Introduction

Teachers deserve loads of credit for dealing with our pubescent behavior and setting our foundation by teaching us writing, reading, history, math and scientific analysis. However, financial education should also be a part of the core curriculum.

Instead, most of us learn about money through The School of Hard Knocks. In that school of life, you get real-world training by spending your money irresponsibly for a number of years before eventually understanding how to be financially responsible.

I wish there was a book like this around when I was a teenager. I took a home economics class that taught me how to fill out a check, but I still ended up bouncing a lot of checks to the point that I almost ended up in jail as a young adult.

I'm not ashamed to admit my mistakes, so others can learn from them. I've overcome my financial missteps to budget the high income I earn as a successful insurance agent and to build my first house on the largest lot in an upper middle class area of my hometown.

With many Americans now struggling through the repercussions of the worst economic climate since the Great Depression of the 1920s and 1930s, I've decided to share my story of financial hardship and the lessons I've learned to teach people, especially teens and young adults, how to develop healthy financial habits that will lead to a comfortable, secure life.

I want you to learn from my mistakes so you won't be burdened down with debt and so you have enough money to enjoy your life. You only have one life to live, and I want you to spend it in financial security.

I know of adults who are in their 50s and 60s struggling to make ends meet and who feel the need to take out home equity loans on their house, which leads to them paying for their mortgage all over again up into their 80s, and some take out reverse mortgages, which robs their children of their house when they die. So the elderly become victims and prey to scam artists and get-rich-quick schemes because they never learned how to properly manage their money instead of letting their money manage them.

Money is managing you when you don't live or eat where you really want and bill collectors are hounding you because you can't pay your obligations. You are managing money when you can fill up your gas tank without scrounging up change in between the seats of your car; when you can on a whim decide to go eat out at your favorite seafood restaurant or steakhouse; and when you get bored with the day-to-day, and you can afford to fly somewhere, take a cruise or buy tickets to see your favorite musician or comedian in another city.

That's the kind of lifestyle I have. I'm not what you would consider to be rich. That is if your standard of rich means I have a million dollars, live in a mansion and drive a $100,000 car. But in my own eyes, I am rich because I'm financially secure enough to do what I want whenever I have an urge to eat somewhere, to go out of town somewhere or to be generous to strangers. To me, that is rich.

I don't want you to be like 63% of Americans over age 65 who are depending on others to take care of them. Some of them plan to work until they drop. Have you been to Wal-Mart, lately? Those elderly greeters and cashiers probably did not learn to budget, save and invest when they were young.

I'm sure you think that won't be you because you plan to be very wealthy someday. Maybe you want to be a doctor, an architect, an accountant, a lawyer or an owner of a successful business or franchise. Or you may want to be a professional athlete. In short, you plan on having a career that generates a lot of money, and I bet you've already thought about the cars and houses you're going to buy and the places you're going to travel to. I daydreamed, too, when I was much younger and still do.

But before you start planning how you're going to spend all of your money, you need to get a handle on your spending by using a budget. If not, you will walk into a high-paying job and spend all of your money, like I once did.

This is because no matter how much money you make, if you don't use it wisely, you won't have any.

Well, you don't need an investment license or an MBA to understand money. But you do need a sound financial education about those greenbacks, so you don't set yourself back in life.

Right now, I want to speak to the young people who are still in school or just entering the workforce. I want you to be prepared when you leave your parents and head out on your own to take care of yourself. You will be faced with decisions on buying groceries to eat, renting a place to stay, paying your cell phone, cable and utility bills, making car payments and purchasing the proper health and life insurance.

These are just some of the things you will have to know how to handle as an adult, so you won't have to crawl back to your parents and other relatives for money like I once had to do even though I was a big-shot local sportswriter.

You also need to learn about budgets, interest rates, FICO scores and credit cards, plus bank accounts, rainy day funds and retirement planning. Don't be overwhelmed. I'm going to patiently break down all of these important areas of personal finances for you, and also explain how you can retire comfortably and never have to depend on your own children, like many retirees.

I know you're thinking this is adult stuff. And you're right. However, adulthood starts as soon as you step foot on your college campus or when you move out of your parents' home. You need to know the dos and don'ts about money, right now. Why?

Well, let's take a glimpse into your future if you don't learn how to handle money now while you're still dependent on someone to take care of you. Shortly after you get to college or move into your new apartment, you're going to get bombarded with credit card offers in the mail. Cool, right? You have plenty of plastic to charge clothes, shoes, movies, video games, trips to Vegas and that annual trip to College Spring Break.

But actually it's not so cool when you experience the aftermath.

You're going to charge your credit cards over the limit. I did. You'll be oblivious to the damage you're doing to your credit score, which determines whether you are approved for a car loan and a house and how much interest you will have to pay on top of the price.

You, like millions of Americans, will likely not have health insurance and so you will rack up emergency room bills that you will decide not to pay, which also ruins your credit score. So when you get into your career and want to buy a nice condo or house, your credit will be too ruined to qualify for a home loan or mortgage, and the marriage to your high school or college sweetheart will hang by a thread because of the strain of debt. The No. 1 reason for divorce is money, so many young marriages fail.

And to top it off, you will not be able to afford to go on any vacations to drown your sorrows because you didn't set a budget when you got that $30,000-$40,000-a-year job out of college, so every penny is allocated to pay bills.

I'm speaking from experience because I had a great paying job out of college, but I had bad credit and couldn't get a car without a co-signer, who is someone who agrees to pay back the loan if you don't. I want you to start off the right way.

I know you don't want to think about your future. You probably just want to party, pledge a Greek organization and enjoy the benefits of being an adult away from home. But knowing how to handle credit cards and medical bills comes with the territory.

You can still have fun, charge cards and go on nice trips, just be smart about it.

I don't want you to leave college and fall into a quarter-life crisis. It's documented that many 25-year-olds suffer an identity crisis similar to a mid-life crisis. So I want to start you on the right course so you don't screw up with money by accumulating $20,000 in credit card debt, completely furnishing your apartment, buying a new car and charging a $5,000 honeymoon on top of a $25,000 wedding to go along with $60,000 in student loans. I did everything, but the student loans and expensive wedding. But now, I'm in the clear.

Struggling with money is a rite of passage that every adult goes through. Ask your parents and your grandparents.

But you can change your destiny.

Please don't put your financial education on hold to party, go to a movie and whatever else teens and young adults do now. You can do those things, just make some time to read through this entire book and refer back to it as you mature through your 20s. Then, check back in your 30s to make sure you're still on the right financial track and give my book to a younger person to make sure they learn to be financially responsible.

I want everyone who reads my book to avoid many of the mistakes that I, and most adults, have made with credit cards, bank accounts, car financing and retirement planning, to name a few. Millions of retired senior citizens are living at or below the U.S. poverty line. That's not exactly the relaxed, pina colada drinking lifestyle you see on TV. Americans of all ages are having money troubles. The United States' wealth is controlled by an exclusive 1% of the more than 300 million Americans.

If you want to be part of that exclusive statistic, be receptive to my advice and put it into practice.

By reading my book, you will be prepared to develop responsible financial habits, and young people won't have to move back home after leaving the nest because they couldn't afford to take care of themselves.

You will learn how to become financially secure. You will learn to use your bank accounts and credit cards responsibly, which will come in handy when you are ready to finance a car or a home. You also will learn how to protect the money you work hard to earn, and you will learn how to plan for a secure retirement. And of course, I will explain how you should treat yourself to enjoy the financial independence you will create for yourself.

If that sounds good, sit back, relax and enjoy the journey I take you on through my financial mishaps in life and the lessons you can take from them so that you may build a secure financial future and have the means to do whatever your heart desires.

Happy reading!

Teneshia LaFaye

My Money Troubles

I was raised by my mother and stepfather until they divorced when I was 12. My birth father, who happens to be a medical surgeon, was never part of my life until recently.

Growing up in the 1980s, I lived a very comfortable life. My mother's hair salon was booming so we ate out at fancy restaurants twice a week, and we went to the movies, roller skating and to the beach every single weekend. My mother took me shopping for new clothes and shoes every other week, so my classmates used to ask me if I was rich. My mother, stepdad and I went to out-of-town fashion shows and hair shows and stayed at 5-star hotels.

So I loved the 80's. My childhood was amazing. However, we didn't have a financial security blanket, so our life began to unravel when my mother divorced my stepdad during my first year in middle school.

Although my mother was the breadwinner, her business slowed down somewhat and she had to take three months off to recuperate from a major surgery. She got behind on her credit card bills, and she depended on my grandfather to pay our living expenses until she got on her feet.

Had my mother been a saver rather than a spender, she wouldn't have had to rely on my grandfather to help us get through a rough patch.

Because I was raised to spend money, I wasn't a saver either when I became an adult, and I also ended up depending on my grandfather to bail me out of financial jams and to pay unexpected expenses.

Unlike in my childhood, I rarely ate at fancy restaurants, and I never went on vacations because it was hard enough to pay my rent, put gas in the tank and buy groceries. I pawned my stuff and got payday advances even though I was earning $33,000-$40,000 annually during five years in my dream job as a sports writer for my hometown newspaper, The Florida Times-Union.

Like you, I was never taught how to be a responsible spender or rather a responsible saver. I was taught how to spend, not how to save. Growing up, I had several cool piggy banks: a ceramic chef pig, a large plastic Coke bottle and a fancy one that separated pennies, dimes, nickels and quarters. I rolled up the coins and had them converted to dollars bills at my mother's bank to spend the money, along with my weekly allowance, at the book store and music store. I used to buy Encyclopedia Brown and Fabulous Five books. My musical preferences were Madonna and Whitney Houston.

I'll bet your childhood wasn't too different from mine. You probably received an allowance and saved your coins to buy candy, music, earrings and things. And like me, you weren't taught financial principles to prepare you to be a responsible adult.

I don't blame my mother or my biological father, who was absent for most of my life and who lost his multiple physician offices and a mega home during the Great Recession. I blame society for not pushing for our schools to teach us how to manage money along with the 3Rs (Reading, Writing and Arithmetic).

When we leave our childhood homes for college and leave college to embark on our careers, we are not properly prepared for the financial responsibilities we will be undertaking.

I was on my new job's payroll for a month and received two paychecks before I graduated college. I give glory to God because many college graduates can't get hired for jobs in their chosen major. Yet I already had a good-paying job at a daily newspaper before walking the aisle to receive my journalism diploma.

I had no student loan debt, so I had a clean slate to begin my financial future, but I didn't use my money wisely and quickly fell into debt with a loan for a new luxury sports coupe and a hefty furniture credit line to furnish every room in my new luxury apartment.

I didn't pay for my new furniture because of a store promotion that eventually led to my financial downfall, and I will tell you the details later so you don't make that mistake.

After accounting for rent, utilities, my car, car insurance, groceries and gas, I had about $100 remaining that I used for automatic deposits for my oldest son's college fund and to buy a burger combo from Wendy's on Friday nights on the way to the weekly high school football games that I covered for the daily newspaper. I also had enough to buy nachos and a Coke at the games and some money to see a $1 movie once a month. I was able to see newly released movies in regular theaters a few times a year.

Aside from my son's college fund, I wasn't saving any money, so when my car broke down and needed repairs, I had to call my grandfather for financial assistance. And when I needed new high performance tires for my sports coupe, I had to ask for money for that, too.

My money troubles were deflating because I was a sports reporter, my face and name were in the newspaper throughout the week. I even had a daily ad running with me and my oldest son Darian, who was 5 at the time.

Although I was making good money and driving a luxury car, my bad financial habits forced me to scatter every other day to acquire money for gas, money for food and sometimes money for going to the movies on the weekend, but never enough for vacations.

Every other week, I went to the grocery store to write checks for cash that I didn't have in the bank. I went to pawn shops to borrow against my jewelry. I used my paycheck as collateral to get $1,000 cash advances every two weeks. I was so embarrassed when a cashier at a pawn shop asked "Don't you write for the paper?" as he handed me a $1,000 advance on my newspaper paycheck. I felt like a crack head.

For at least a year, a relative and I wrote $30-$70 personal checks to each other to get us by until our next payday. But one day, a security officer at my credit union pulled me aside and gave me a slap on the wrist. But he warned that next time, handcuffs would be slapped on me because I was taking part in check kiting, which is writing worthless checks with no money in the bank for someone else to obtain cash.

However, I continued to use the grocery store and cash advances to make ends meet. It got so bad that while working on a front-page newspaper story that eventually won a national and state journalism award, I was interrupted by a bill collector who threatened to repossess my car. Eventually, it was repossessed and my oldest son was late to school while we got a ride to my grandfather's to get money to have my car released.

I financed four cars in my 20s, but I never paid either of them off. I traded in each one for a newer one and had each outstanding balance added onto the newer car. I struggled to make my car payments and keep in mind I made $40,000 a year. I shouldn't have been struggling so badly.

Every three or four months, I knocked back my monthly car payments to the end of the loan in order to skip a payment. Eventually all those pushed back payments added another year or two of having to make payments, which meant paying even more interest on my car.

Basically, I was working to pay for my cars.

Thank God I don't live like that anymore. Since learning how to use money wisely, I've taken my family across the country to New York and Los Angeles a couple times and on cruises to Alaska and the Bahamas.

I used to be so broke that I couldn't afford a two-hour road trip to Orlando. Now, I've taken both of my sons to Orlando a couple dozen times in the last three years.

Before, I wasn't living within my means. I was living above my means, which is typical of Americans.

I told you my story so that you can understand how your life will be if you don't learn to manage your money now rather than later. Maybe you've had your own personal failure with finances. Hopefully, the lessons I teach you set the foundation for you to be more responsible with money.

Work At Something You Enjoy

It's hard to get a good-paying job, and even any job in this harsh economic climate. So some people feel forced to work in a less than ideal job.

I want to caution you about working on a job just to earn a paycheck. I'm sure you've heard the saying to get a job you love and you will never work a day in your life.

It's no fun when you hate your job. You start thinking about how much you don't want to go to work hours before it's time for you to clock in. You start coming in late or you make excuses not to come in at all and you end up getting fired. I know because I did it.

This is a big mistake because, like it or not, you were hired to do a good job and your livelihood likely depends on it. Besides, you will need your former bosses as references for future jobs, and you may need to turn around and go back when no one else will hire you.

Save yourself the headache and get a job you enjoy.

Because I was unhappy with what I was doing, I went from job to job during high school and my first couple years in college. Finally, I decided to make the most of my quick typing skills to settle into part-time data entry work during my last two years of college.

But I wish YouTube had been around back in the early 1990s when I was a teen. Because my passion was writing poetry and rhyming, I used to make rap videos on my uncle's camcorder. If YouTube existed, I could have been discovered online like Justin Bieber and Soulja Boy.

By the end of my sophomore year of college, I had fallen in love with watching football and basketball and chose to major in journalism to parlay my writing talents and newfound sports love into a career as a newspaper sportswriter. I made good money as a sportswriter, won several awards and enjoyed interviewing the likes of sports legends Michael Jordan, Cal Ripken and Roger Staubach.

But then I felt compelled to work in a profession that helps make people's lives better, so I took a $10,000 pay cut to be a high school English teacher and then I moved onto insurance, where I get paid very well to help the disabled and the elderly apply for Medicaid and lower their prescription and medical costs.

I said all of that to say that you should find a job that interests you or at least uses your talents. While growing up, my mother used to style her friends' hair in my grandfather's house, and she used to tell her friends that she was going to own a hair salon someday. She ended up opening the first black hair salon in an upscale area of my hometown. Now, there is a black hair salon on almost every block.

If you like shopping, you should get a job at one of your favorite clothing stores. You'll make money while enjoying the atmosphere and you will get discounts on new styles. If you are reliable and go out of your way to make a good impression, you may be offered a position to be a buyer for a major retail store or you may use your connections to launch your own clothing line or to start a boutique that leads to your own chain of stores.

If you like movies, work at a movie theater. How cool would it be to be paid and see all the latest movies for free? You may move up to management, like a childhood friend of mine who began working at a theatre in high school and continued while away in college and now she runs the busiest mega theatre in town.

If you are into gadgets, work at a cell phone or electronics store. If you like cars, work at a car wash or accessories shop or start your own mobile-detailing business. You also may want to pursue a degree in engineering and start your own company that specializes in home entertainment systems, like a guy I knew in high school.

In this tough economy with adults competing with teenagers for jobs, you made need to use the talent that God gave you and make money from it.

When my oldest son Darian was 5 years old, a coworker asked him what he wanted to be when he grows up. He said, "a boss." And now he's his own boss. He taught himself how to design websites when he was 10 years old. Small business owners pay him to design web sites for them. I paid him to create my national blog, www.mytensense.com. Darian also dresses very well, so he partnered with one of his best friends to create a fashion rating site, www.Faddest.com, that he plans to be profitable enough for him to pursue his third passion, designing office buildings and hotels like Donald Trump. He's in school now studying architectural design.

Maybe you're not good with computers, but you have other God-given talents. Figure out which ones are profitable and start a business around that talent.

If you're living with your parents, be like my son, and partner up with your friends to start a business, such as babysitting or a lawn service. You also may be able to fall back on your parents, other relatives, neighbors and people they refer for you to do unwanted household chores or handy work. I know young people who baby sit in their parents' homes, who go around washing cars and who offer their craftiness for home improvement services.

My oldest son also makes extra cash from selling his and his friends' stuff on EBay and Amazon. By the way, my youngest son Dominick, an elementary school student, makes money to save in his piggy bank and bank savings account by finding loose change around the house and getting money for his birthdays and report cards.

When I was a teen, I made extra money from selling candy and posters of popular young actors and entertainers that I pulled from teen magazines.

Whatever job you decide to pursue, make sure you like it and can be committed to doing a good job because you will need references, or if it's your business, you will want referrals for more customers to help you reach your professional goals. As an insurance agent, I get half of my customers off referrals each month. There's no way I would reach my sales goals if I didn't do a good job and get referrals from satisfied clients.

Quiz 1

Choose the best answer

1) You should get a job that you _________.
   A. hate
   B. enjoy
   C. pays $8 per hour

2) If you like gadgets, you should work at a _________.
   A. movie theater
   B. flower shop
   C. cell phone store

3) If no company will hire you, you should _________.
   A. stay home and play video games
   B. hang out with friends
   C. get paid for your talents

Don't Spend Your Whole Paycheck

Let's say you've found a job you enjoy, and you're receiving some nice paychecks. I bet you already know how you're going to spend the money before every payday.

If so, you're not alone. Most people live paycheck to paycheck because they already have plans for their earnings before payday. So their money is already mentally spent before they cash their paycheck in, and sometimes the money is already allocated two to three pay periods ahead.

I was one of them. I got my first couple of paychecks in my chosen field a month before college graduation and I used them to lease a new luxury apartment and to purchase new furniture for all of the rooms. I thought "Well, I take home $900 every other week, so let me tally my expenses and see what else I can buy. And hopefully I will have enough remaining for a movie or to eat out once a week." After calculating my expenses and my new debt purchases, I ended up with $100 left over each month and used some of it to deposit money into the college fund of my only child at the time.

I had a little money to buy a burger combo, nachos and a Coke as my weekly ritual for the Friday night high school games I covered as the full-time high school sports beat writer for the local newspaper. And thank goodness for the $1 movie theatre, where I would go once or twice a month.

I had fallen into the trap of living paycheck to paycheck and I was only 21 years old. I had just enough money to get me by until my next payday. God forbid an unexpected expense occurred, and it often did.

I'm sharing this with you because I don't want you to make the same mistakes and join the majority of Americans who live paycheck to paycheck. It's been said that most U.S. workers are a paycheck away from being poor because they don't budget their earnings nor do they make a habit of saving, which I will discuss in a later chapter. So if they lose their jobs, they won't have money to afford basic necessities.

Many adults learned this the hard way or never learned their lesson and they're struggling to get by today. I bet you know several people who are struggling financially. I've heard of adults who go to their kids to borrow money. I'm not trying to make fun, but you don't want that to be you when you get older and have children of your own.

You really shouldn't get into the habit of spending your entire paycheck because unforeseen events will happen in your life.

In my early to mid-20s, I used to lean on my grandfather if I needed a new car battery or new high performance tires for the luxury sports coupe I foolishly bought myself after I graduated college to one-up a co-worker who had just bought a new sports utility vehicle.

I had no choice but to ask my granddad for money because I lived paycheck to paycheck and didn't set aside any money. My granddad never made me feel bad about borrowing money from him, but my mother always told me to be financially independent and to never depend on anyone for money.

So I never felt right asking my granddad for money. It wasn't a good feeling being broke and having to ask him or a friend for money to pay a bill or to buy groceries.

It's also deflating when there's something you really want to do, but you don't have any money to do it.

Don't get into the habit of spending your entire paycheck because you won't have the money to hang out with your friends, to buy something you really want or just to buy a couple shirts or accessories to spice up your wardrobe. Or maybe you will want to have money to buy a ticket when your favorite musician comes to town.

But if you spend your entire paycheck, you will have to ask your parent, a sibling, a friend or someone else for money when you want or need something. And who likes begging for money? Part of being independent is not depending on others for handouts, but responsibly handling your finances.

So don't go spending all your money and then have to go and borrow money for your expenses. Having your own money gives you a lot of freedom because people can't threaten to take things away or to stop paying for your privileges.

This is important to learn at an early age because you don't want to be an independent adult and have to crawl back to your family to borrow money for rent, food or your car note because you spent the money on unimportant things. I actually had to move back in with my family when I was an award-winning sports writer because I couldn't afford the lifestyle created from spending my entire $40,000 annual salary.

I don't want you to be in that uncomfortable position of not being able to afford basic necessities and having to move back in with family.

So do yourself a big favor and don't spend your whole paycheck. Learn to manage your money and live within your means, so that you can pay all of your responsibilities and when you really want something or want to do something special, you have the money to do it and won't have to wait on a handout.

Quiz 2

True or False

1) Many Americans are one paycheck away from being poor. *True or False*

2) You should spend all of your money and borrow more from your family and friends. *True or False*

3) Unexpected things can happen, so don't spend your entire paycheck. *True or False*

How Much You Make Doesn't Matter

If you've ever worked hard on your job, the thought has likely crossed your mind. You think, "If I can only get a promotion and make more money. Then, I can pay all my bills and have money to buy whatever I want."

Most working adults have thought the same thing, even me. But it's very difficult to get ahead of your bills and live the life of your dreams because the more money you make, the more money you spend.

It's not how much you make, it's how much you keep. You can make $20,000 a year and live an extraordinary life.

Actors and professional athletes make millions of dollars and hit the lottery every time they get paid, but many of them end up bankrupt just like most lottery winners.

I've read that people who win $1 million or less in the lottery are broke within a year, and it takes less than 10 years for an individual to blow through a major jackpot, such as $100 million or more.

Lottery winners are a lot like celebrities and top professional athletes. Many celebs and pro athletes buy up multiple lavish houses around the world and drive expensive cars. But as soon as their career takes a dive, so does their lifestyle and many of them end up broke.

Mike Tyson earned more than $300 million in his boxing career and ended up filing for bankruptcy. During a 2010 interview, the former world heavyweight champion said, "I'm totally destitute and broke."

Former NBA scoring leader Allen Iverson's bank account recently was seized because he couldn't pay an $800,000 jewelry debt. He once earned $154 million in NBA salary alone.

Rapper Lil Wayne has made millions from his multi-platinum records and off of the successful records of Nicki Minaj and Drake, two artists on Wayne's Young Money Entertainment record label. Yet, Lil Wayne has had more than $6 million in tax liens in the last three years for failure to pay taxes on his income.

Michael Jackson had a half billion dollar fortune that he squandered with his extravagant lifestyle, and Whitney Houston signed a $100 million contract with Arista Records in 2001 after already making millions selling 170 million records, among the highest record sales of all-time for a pop artist, and starring in and producing movies. But after their popularity faded, the King of Pop and The Voice squandered their fortunes and were rumored to be broke at the time of their deaths.

Former Pro Bowl NFL receiver Terrell Owens once signed a $25 million contract with the Dallas Cowboys after already getting $49 million from the Philadelphia Eagles. He had a beautiful Atlanta mansion that was featured on MTV Cribs, a popular show in which celebrities take viewers on a tour of their homes. But when T.O. became unemployed by the NFL in 2011, his Atlanta mansion quickly went into foreclosure and he was threatened with jail time for being behind $20,000 in child support payments.

Recently Warren Sapp, a retired Pro Bowl defensive tackle and analyst for the NFL Network, has gone bankrupt. Sapp once signed the richest NFL contract for a defensive player, $36 million, with the Oakland Raiders after previously making millions with Tampa Bay. Yet he declared bankruptcy after owing $6.7 million, almost $300,000 more than his assets. He also owed hundreds of thousands in back child support payments.

I'm not trying to judge Sapp or any of the other celebrities who have lost their fortunes. But their loss is our gain because we can learn many lessons from their financial downfall. In hindsight, I bet they wish they would have banked their millions and settled into a normal upper middle class lifestyle. That way they would have preserved their wealth and it would have allowed them and their families to live comfortably for generations. Instead, many of them live like kings and queens until their money runs out and some of them become paupers who turn to drugs and alcohol to drown their sorrows.

The lesson you should learn from celebrities is that it doesn't matter how much you make. It matters how much money you hold on to. Don't get caught up in how much money you make. Learn how to make the most out of what you earn.

I know that now, but I didn't know it when I was struggling to survive off $28,000 a year in my first job out of college or when I continued to struggle while earning $40,000 a year in my mid-20s. Making that kind of money, I had no business being broke, borrowing money for car repairs and being threatened to have my car repossessed. And I used to think, "If only I made more money."

But the amount of money I made wouldn't have mattered if I had a plan for how to budget and save my money rather than spending it all up and not having any money when the unexpected occurred.

Don't be like Mike!

A celebrity example of the consequences of living above your means:

Mike Tyson earned $300 million in his boxing career and ended up filing for bankruptcy. During a 2010 interview, the former world heavyweight champion said, "I'm totally destitute and broke."

Quiz 3

Choose the best answer

1) The more money you make, the more money you _________.
   A. have
   B. spend
   C. give

2) Many celebrities could prevent going broke if they _________.
   A. give more money to charity
   B. settle into a middle class lifestyle
   C. spend lavishly

3) It's not how much you make, it's how much you _________.
   A. spend
   B. keep
   C. borrow

Live On A Budget

Regardless of the amount of money you earn, you worked hard for it and shouldn't just blow it all on payday. You're not playing with Monopoly money. This is real money with real value.

You should plan how to be a responsible spender by making a budget that includes buying necessities, saving money for a rainy day, treating yourself and giving. Most importantly, you should plan to live within your means, meaning you spend less than you earn.

By making a budget to live within your means, you will be able to afford all of your basic necessities. You won't have to beg, borrow and plead to cover your rent for the month or to get out of a financial jam from an unexpected expense. You will be able to afford to treat yourself to a mini-shopping spree, and you may take a nice vacation or splurge on front-row seats to see your favorite musician in concert. All of this will be possible if you make a plan to spend your money responsibly.

Your budget should adhere to my 60-20-10-10 rule©. This calls for spending 60% of your take-home pay on necessities, saving 20%, using 10% as your allowance and giving away 10%. If you don't want to give away as much, knock it down to 5% and add an additional 5% to your savings or allowance. Don't tack on more living expenses.

Your take-home pay is what you actually receive on your paycheck after payroll taxes are taken out.

Basic necessities could be rent or a mortgage, gas, groceries, and a cell phone bill. Shopping, manicures and car detailing aren't necessities.

By following my 60-20-10-10 rule©, you will never live paycheck to paycheck like most people. You will have money for a rainy day. You will be able to treat yourself, and you will be a blessing to people in need.

Let me give you an example of living by my 60-20-10-10 rule©.

If your take-home pay is $1,000 per month, the rule calls for your necessities, such as rent, transportation, groceries, electric, cell phone and cable bills to be no more than $600 per month. You should save $200 per month. Give yourself a $100 allowance and tithe $100 to a charity and/or your church.

As you move up in your profession, your take-home pay may climb to $3,500 per month, so your necessities should only be $2,100, you should save $700, have a $350 allowance and give away $350. Remember if you don't want to be as gracious, you can adjust the percentages, but not to add more living expenses. Your allowance would probably be for shopping and eating at nice restaurants, and your giving may be to your church, a needy family member or your child's college fund.

The two biggest expenses you're likely to have are paying for your residence and your car payments. These two expenses can cause a heavy financial burden and are the most hurtful when you cannot manage them because you could be evicted from your home or have your car repossessed.

Of the 60% for expenses, I recommend that your rent or mortgage not be more than half, meaning no more than 30% of your take-home pay. For young people right out of school, I suggest getting a roommate if you have to or rent your old room in your family's home. It's better to live within or below your means and have the money to get out of the house to enjoy life rather than having to scrounge up money for rent and having no money for extracurricular activities.

When it's time for you to buy a car, you shouldn't finance it for more than half your annual salary. So if you make $15,000 per year, you should get a car that costs $7,500 or less. If you make $24,000 per year, you shouldn't get a car for more than $12,000. If you begin making $40,000 per year, you should get a car for no more than $20,000. And if you ever pull in $100,000, you can afford a $50,000 luxury sedan. But don't you dare buy a car if you don't have a rainy day fund. Also, don't decide to buy a new car if your transmission goes out because a transmission is only $2,000-$5,000. A new car will cost at least four times that, plus interest. I know a couple who was living above their means in a big, beautiful house and struggling to pay their bills. They got behind on their mortgage, and they still financed a $30,000 car because they didn't want to pay a couple thousand in repairs for their old car, which was paid off. So now they're using money they really can't afford to spend on their new car, and they borrow money from one of their children to make ends meet. As far as their beautiful house, they are trying to stay out of foreclosure.

I've been guilty of trading in a car rather than pay for the necessary repairs, but that's an old habit that I have since broken. It just doesn't make since to tack on tens of thousands of debt by buying a new car to avoid a car repair that costs a few hundred or maybe a couple thousand dollars. But many people do it because they haven't saved for a rainy day to be able to afford major car repairs.

It's also very common for people to buy cars they can't afford. Judging from the cars on the road, I'm willing to bet that most people finance a car equal to or more than their annual salary. I'm sure they also rent an apartment that is more than half of their take-home pay. They probably scramble around trying to come up with money for rent, groceries and gas, and they can't wait until tax season to get a tax refund check in order to catch up on bills and buy objects of their desire.

And if an unexpected expense comes up, they are out of gas and have to beg, borrow and plead with their family and friends for money. Or worse, they hold up a sign on the side of the road, asking for food and money.

You don't have to live like that. If you learn to live on a budget early in life, you will save yourself a lot of headaches and avoid struggling from paycheck to paycheck and being burdened down with living expenses and credit card debt.

Living on a budget will make your life less stressful and you can afford to get away or go shopping when life becomes overwhelming.

If your finances are overextended and you're in a lot of debt, you should downsize your life by cutting down your expenses and making a plan to pay off your debt. In this case, 80% of your take-home pay should be used toward expenses with the mindset of paying off your debt and cutting down unnecessary living expenses.

You should save 10% for a rainy day, give yourself a 5% allowance and give away 5%. Then, when your debt is eliminated, with maybe the exception of your house, and your living expenses are reasonable, you should be able to live by my 60-20-10-10 rule© going forward.

If I would have lived by the 60-20-10-10 rule© when I graduated from college, I would have saved at least $360 per month to have plenty of money set aside to pay for my own tires instead of asking my grandfather to buy them. I also would have been able to go away on vacations and would have enjoyed a $180 allowance to see new movies in theaters and to dine at fancy restaurants a couple times per month instead of settling for a burger combo and a $1 movie.

But now, I'm a testament to the 60-20-10-10 rule© and use it to live within my means and to drive a car worth only 10% of my salary. I can afford to go shopping for new shoes or new outfits to spice up my wardrobe whenever I want, but I shop sporadically because saving is more important to me. When I'm tired of cooking at home, I can afford to eat at a nice restaurant without skipping payment on a bill or using gas money. When life gets boring, I can leave town for the weekend.

You can plan to have a similar lifestyle if you set a budget based on my 60-20-10-10 rule© and follow through on it. Or you can be like the many who don't live by a budget and struggle from paycheck to paycheck.

60-20-10-10 Rule©

- 60% Living expenses (rent, mortgage, electric, groceries, gas, phone, TV, car payments, insurance, credit card bills)
- 20% Savings (rainy day, retirement, 401K, future goals, vacations)
- 10% Allowance (restaurants, movies, concerts, activities)
- 10% Giving (church, charity, family, friends)

Quiz 4

True or False

Your budget should consist of necessities, saving, treating yourself and giving. *True or False*

The two biggest expenses in your budget are likely to be shopping and car repairs. *True or False*

If you live by my 60-20-10-10 rule©, you will never live paycheck to paycheck. *True or False*

Save For A Rainy Day

You carry a spare tire in your trunk in case you have a flat tire, and you probably keep a jacket or a sweater in your car in case it gets chilly. You also may have an umbrella tucked away in case it rains.

So you should have a financial security blanket in case an unexpected expense comes up. You should have at least six months to one year of living expenses tucked away in case you lose your job or have a financial emergency. You will certainly need money for car maintenance and repairs, so you won't feel forced to trade into a new car and take on tens of thousands in new debt.

To figure out how much money you need to save for a rainy day, multiply your monthly living expenses by 6 or 12. So if your monthly necessities are $600 per month, you should have at least $3,600-$7,200 saved. If your expenses are $1,000 per month, you should have $6,000-$12,000 stashed away.

However, underneath your mattress, on your dresser or some secret spot around your home aren't safe places to stash your cash because they leave you financially vulnerable to burglary or a disaster, such as a house fire, to lose what you worked hard to save.

I know a middle-aged man who kept his money in a safe that was stolen, likely by one of his nephew's friends who walked by the safe almost every day.

I know an older lady who keeps her money underneath her mattress, which could burn up in a house fire. And what if someone finds her secret stash spot and steals the money she worked hard to save?

A piggy bank is a good option for loose change that can be rolled up and deposited later at your bank or credit union, or your change can be deposited into a coin machine at a grocery store to be converted into dollar bills. I had several piggy banks as a child, even a cool one that separated pennies, nickels, dimes and quarters into columns. However, piggy banks aren't real banks because they don't pay interest.

Interest is the percentage of your money that the bank will add onto the money you've deposited to build up your balance. The higher the interest rate, the more your money grows in your savings account.

Banks and credit unions add interest to the money you deposit in exchange for your money sitting in your account to be included in the financial institution's total holdings from all account holders in order to offer credit cards and loans for mortgages, cars, college tuition and other major purchases.

However, banks and credit unions are now giving minimal interest rates for savings accounts that are less than half of a percent. So you are likely to earn only 10 to 50 cents in interest every month if you deposit $100 into a savings account, which translates to only $1-$6 extra in your account at the end of the year.

It may not seem like much, but that's just per $100 in your account. If you keep making deposits every pay period and leave the money alone, the bank will continue to add interest as a thank you for keeping your money in there for them to loan out. Your bank's modest interest is better than your money collecting dust around your home and being vulnerable to a hazard or burglary. And as you continue to save part of each paycheck, your balance will grow from $100 to $1,000, then to $2,000 and more to be there for a rainy day and your other financial goals.

Regardless of the low interest earnings, I recommend a savings account for your 6-12 month rainy day fund so you can easily access your money in an emergency and can avoid a financial penalty for withdrawing money too soon from a CD, an IRA or your job's 401K. In a vibrant economy, a money market savings account usually gives a higher interest rate than a regular savings account, but savings and money markets are giving comparably low rates in this down economy. So you should lean toward a savings account because it usually only requires a $5 initial deposit versus the $100-$500 necessary to open a money market account.

But you should shop around for the best savings and money market interest rates in your area by visiting www.bankrate.com or www.interest.com.

Some financial institutions are making up for their low savings interest rates by offering reward programs for using your debit card that is tied to your checking account. For instance, if you use your debit card to make a $4.63 purchase, your bank may add the difference to the next dollar, 37 cents, into your savings account. So every time you make a purchase from your checking account using your debit card, your savings account grows. Ask your bank if this program is offered.

To make saving easier, you should talk to your job's payroll representative about automatically having at least 10% of your paycheck sent to your savings account or you can manually transfer the money from your checking to your savings every payday through an online account at your bank.

Make saving fun by visualizing how independently secure you will feel when you've filled your rainy day fund and by setting other financial goals, such as a cruise to Alaska, a 60-inch TV, a down payment for a car or new furniture.

I would recommend having multiple savings accounts for your various goals. Your banker can help you create various sub accounts within your main savings account. So you may have money market and savings accounts for a rainy day, for a car, for vacations and for furniture.

With the exception of the rainy day fund, you may want to consider opening a couple of certificate of deposit (CD) accounts for goals that are more than six months out because CD rates are higher than savings and money market account rates. A CD is a type of savings account, except you cannot withdraw your money from it until the period ends, so be sure you don't need the money during that time period for an emergency. You usually need $500-$1,000 to open a CD, and you can get an account for 3 months, 6 months, 9 months, one year or longer. The longer the CD period is the higher the interest rate you receive for your money to grow. However, if you withdraw your money prematurely, you will be charged an early withdrawal penalty.

Unlike savings and money market rates that are averaging less than a percent, CD rates currently are at 1% to 1.9%. But to get the highest CD rates, you have to lock your money up for five years. You may feel it's worth it because you can earn $1-2 per month for every $100 in a CD rather than 50 cents or less for every $100 in a savings account.

To find the best available CD interest rates in your area, go to www.bankrate.com or www.interest.com. Remember, you also can use those sites to compare savings and money market account rates.

Once you start saving money, don't depend on it for your living expenses or your allowance. That shouldn't be a problem if you live by the 60-20-10-10 rule© I discussed in the previous chapter. So keep socking your money away for that rainy day and for your financial goals.

Quiz 5

Choose the best answer

1) A _________ keeps your money safe and interest is added to help your money grow.
   A. piggy bank
   B. savings account
   C. safe

2) An interest rate _________.
   A. adds money to your savings account
   B. subtracts a fee from your savings account
   C. has no effect on your savings account

3) A bank CD is a _________.
   A. disc with several songs
   B. savings account that locks in a set interest rate to grow your money for a specific number of months or years
   C. percentage of your money the bank will add onto the money you deposited

Treat Yourself

What good is working and making money, if you can't spend it on things that make you happy?

Don't you work to be able to buy things that make you happy?

And if you are budgeting and saving your money, you deserve to spend it sometimes. You deserve to treat yourself. That's why earlier I mentioned that you should pay yourself an allowance that is 10% of your take-home pay.

I know, sometimes you need a break from your normal life. So instead of cooking or getting the usual pizza, you may want to go out to a fancy restaurant. You may get tired of wearing the same rotation of clothes and may want to spruce up your wardrobe by buying a few new shirts and a new pair of shoes. Or you may want to go out of town for the weekend to re-charge.

Go for it.

You have to treat yourself sometimes to reward yourself for working hard and for being responsible with your money. Just don't touch your rainy day fund and don't spend more than 10% of your savings, unless you have a specific account for your treat, such as a sub account for vacations.

So if you want a $400 designer bag or a $200 pair of sneakers, go ahead. If you want to order a $25-50 plate at a fancy restaurant, do it. But remember to leave your rainy day fund for emergencies.

And keep in mind that you are treating yourself. Don't make a habit of purchasing high ticket items and eating at fancy restaurants. It's no longer a treat if you do it all the time or every week.

It's not OK to spend every paycheck on costly treats unless it fits into your allowance. If you do, eventually you will start draining your savings accounts and possibly your rainy day fund to support your bad spending habits. So don't create a spending habit. Treat it as a treat.

Believe me a treat is more exciting and rewarding. My oldest son Darian loves chocolate covered strawberries, but he only buys them on special occasions. If he bought them every week, he would probably be sick of them, and he would likely lose his washboard stomach.

Darian is also a snazzy dresser, which is why he created the social fashion rating site, www.Faddest.com. But even he admits that it's not very exciting buying new clothes every week. Besides excessive shopping becomes an expense that knocks you off your budget and may force you to start dipping into your savings or limiting your savings deposits to look like a million bucks instead of having a million bucks saved.

Now, I'm talking to those of you who want to be independent by spending your own money, not other people's money.

You also shouldn't make a habit out of visiting expensive restaurants. The food just doesn't melt in your mouth as well as when you go less often. Instead, treat yourself by going to a pricey eatery once a month or every other month to keep your excitement high.

One of my favorite restaurants is Red Lobster because I just love seafood. There was a time when I took my family there on special occasions, as many families do. But when I began to prosper financially, we began going to Red Lobster multiple times in the same month. So it stopped being an enjoyable experience for me and my family. We actually agreed to being sick of Red Lobster. I didn't mind if I never went there again in my life.

So don't fall into the habit of overindulging because you would be robbing yourself of the joy of getting a treat every now and then to break away from your dull routine.

As far as trips, it's OK to take an impromptu weekend trip for a couple hundred bucks to recharge your batteries. But it's best to plan your major vacations and getaways at the beginning of each year. You may want to have a special savings account for vacations. By planning early, you can shop for price deals, request the necessary off days at work, and you are able to pre-plan activities to make the most of your vacation. Most importantly, you can make sure the trip doesn't disrupt your budget and savings goals.

After all, the point of a treat is to enjoy the life you have created by sticking to your budget and saving goals.

Quiz 6

True or False

1) If you work hard to budget and save your money, you should treat yourself sometimes. *True or False*

2) It's a treat to buy something new every week. *True or False*

3) It's OK to overindulge by treating yourself all the time. *True or False*

Use A Checking Account Responsibly

If you have a job, you should open a checking account for several reasons.

It's better to deposit your paycheck into your checking account and have access to all of your money rather than cashing it and having some of the funds put on hold by your bank for a few days or paying fees to cash your check at a check-cashing store.

You also can enroll in direct deposit on your job and your money is automatically deposited into your checking account. So you can wake up on payday and log in to your account on your bank's web site and see how much money you earned. It beats waiting in a long line at a check-cashing store or a bank to get your money. And at some companies, your paycheck is in your bank account a day or two before payday.

By having a checking account, you can sign up for a check card/debit card and use it to make purchases so you're not loaded down with money in your wallet that entices you to spend it all and leaves you vulnerable to thieves.

You also can write checks for your bills or enroll in automatic bank draft or bill pay to automatically send off your monthly payments, so you never get a late penalty for paying past the due date. Plus, it's a good idea to write a check for church tithes and offerings and contributions to your favorite charity. Then, you'll have a record in order to have tax write-offs, which is less of your money owed to Uncle Sam and it may lead to a bigger tax refund check when you file your taxes at the beginning of every year.

Checks also are a necessity to obtain health and life insurance because you usually need to write a check for the first month's premium and give the agent a voided check for your monthly premiums to automatically be taken from your checking account in order to avoid a lapse in coverage.

You also can use a checking account to track your spending online or through the monthly statements in the mail to make sure you are being true to your budget. By accessing your account online, you can see a listing of all of your check card purchases and each check written that has cleared your account.

The biggest reward of having a checking account is, by establishing a good relationship with your bank, you may be offered low-interest loans, which means less money to pay back, on a house, car or some other loan. With your bank's backing, when it's time to buy a car or a house, you can bring your pre-approval letter and negotiate the deal that you want. Because you have the money already in your hands, the salesperson only has to meet your needs.

Now that you see the benefits of opening a checking account, let me tell you about the pitfalls.

One downside is that some banks charge a monthly fee for a checking account, usually $7-$15 per month. You can avoid a bank's monthly checking account fee if you sign up for direct deposit of your paycheck or you keep a specific minimum balance, such as $100. Ordinarily, banks don't charge a monthly fee if you're a student.

Usually credit unions don't charge members a monthly fee for a checking account, so try opening an account there first. But you usually need to be referred by a family member or a friend who already has an account at a credit union. It's worth the hassle of finding relatives to refer you to their credit union to save on those monthly fees.

Another potential problem with a checking account is that you may use your check/debit card so much that you lose track of your spending and don't have enough money in the bank to cover additional purchases. If you don't have the money to cover purchases, you are charged an overdraft fee, usually $28-38, for each purchase after you go over the balance in your account.

You need to keep track of your expenses by daily reviewing your account online or by writing each purchase in your checkbook registry.

If you're not monitoring your spending, it's easy to forget that you used your check card to purchase a couple CDs or a video game for $30 on your way home from school or work. So you foolishly use your check card again to spend another $30 at a restaurant and a movie theater. So if you only have $30 in your checking account, both of those charges will go through to leave you with a -$30 balance and your bank will likely add a $28 or $38 NSF (insufficient funds) fee to bring your balance to -$58 or -68.

But for the most part, it's great to have a checking account for the reasons I mentioned earlier. To avoid those NSF fees, sign up for free overdraft protection so when you go over the limit, the bank will move the money over from your savings account and a small fee may be charged, depending on the bank. But don't rely on overdraft protection because you will siphon away your rainy day savings.

One bad check can cause your checking account to go from $200 to $0 in minutes. I know you want to buy a $400 designer purse or maybe a $200 pair of sneakers. But if you only have $60 in your checking account, you shouldn't write a check for the purchase even if you're about to get a paycheck in 2 or 3 days. If you write a $200 check with only $60 in your bank account and you don't have the full amount to cover your check if that check comes through in 1-2 days, the bank will slap you with an NSF fee, bringing your account down to a $22 or a $32 balance. And the check might be run through a second time to leave you with nothing and the store still hasn't received the $200 that you owe. So the store will report you to the state attorney, and you will have to pay the amount on the bad check you wrote, plus government fees. If you don't pay up, you will go to jail. So as the saying goes, "don't write checks you can't cash".

I had my share of state attorney's letters ordering me to make good on checks or face the consequences of jail time. I paid up, so I never went behind bars.

It's important to use caution when writing checks or using your debit card. What if you need gas money? You can be stuck arguing with the gas station cashier that you have money in the bank, but you don't realize you're broke because you forgot that you wrote a $50 check at the hair salon a few days ago and that check has already cleared your account leaving you with no money in your checking account to pay for gas.

So use your checkbook registry to keep track of the checks you write. This way you will have money for gas and lunch when you need it and no one has to threaten your freedom.

Of course, if you're living by my budget formula, you will always have money for gas and your checks will be honored at the bank.

Quiz 7

Choose the best answer

1) When you get your paycheck, you should get it cashed at a _________.
   A. check-cashing store
   B. bank or credit union
   C. cash advance store

2) Direct deposit is when _________ your checking account.
   A. your bills are automatically taken out of
   B. your paycheck is automatically put into
   C. your bank or credit union adds interest to

3) NSF means _________.
   A. National Savings Federation
   B. insufficient funds
   C. non-savings fund

Quiz 8

True or False

1) It's OK to write a check if you're going to deposit the money in a few days. *True or False*

2) You will not pay a fee for a bounced check. *True or False*

3) Don't write checks that you can't cash. *True or False*

Be Careful with Credit

So where do you go when your paycheck isn't enough and your parents and other family members won't bail you out?

Well, a lot of people just charge their credit cards or go to loan sharks, such as title companies and cash advance stores. Recently, I was at a tax office and noticed at least 12 adults in a half-hour time frame visiting the payday loan place next door for a short-term loan to pay their bills and for spending money. I know why they were there because I used to be one of them.

I don't recommend credit cards or payday loans if you're in a financial crunch because odds are you won't have the money to pay off the credit card for a while and payday loans are a vicious cycle that will have you giving up your entire paycheck every other week. And definitely stay away from title companies that take over ownership of your car or home if you don't repay your short-term loan.

You shouldn't borrow any kind of money until you have saved for your rainy day fund. I believe this for two reasons.

First, you shouldn't be borrowing money for a big emergency because more than likely you don't have the money to quickly pay it back and you will be on the hook for the money you borrowed, plus extra interest payments. Interest is bad when you owe money because you owe your original loan amount, plus a percentage in interest. Secondly, if you don't have any assets like a loaded savings account, it is unlikely that a bank would offer you a credit card, and if so, it will probably have a high interest rate. But if you have that rainy day fund, your bank will be offering you the best interest rates to accept their credit cards, and a low interest rate means less money for you to pay back.

Credit cards are preferable to going to title companies and cash advance stores.

With title companies, you get a high-interest, short-term loan, and you give up the rights to your car if you fail to pay back the money you owe.

Many people turn to cash advance stores and give up their entire paycheck for a short-term loan. You can get $100-$500 and sometimes $1,000, but you have to pay back the cash advance store with as high as 300% interest on your next pay check. This starts a dangerous cycle because you have to give away your entire paycheck to pay back the cash advance place, and then get another payday loan to pay your bills. Then, you pay the loan back a second time when you get paid and get a third loan to pay your bills and on and on. And a lot of people never get out of this cash advance cycle.

I fell into the cash advance trap for years. I would give up my entire $1,100 biweekly paycheck and re-advance for $1,000 to pay my bills. I was so embarrassed when a clerk at a pawn shop asked me if I was a writer for the local newspaper as he gave me a $1,000 cash advance. Eventually, I mustered the nerve to ask for my grandfather's help. After he bailed me out of the cash advance cycle, I vowed to never get another payday loan and I haven't since 2003.

Credit cards are a better way to make purchases when you're short on cash.

First, you should know the difference between credit cards and charge cards. When you use a credit card, you may carry a balance for months and years, but you are expected to make a minimum payment on your balance each month. Part of your minimum payment is an interest rate, which is a pre-determined fee the creditor gives you for the privilege of borrowing money.

However with a charge card, you have no interest to pay on purchases because you have to pay off the full balance from your purchases for the month when you receive a bill at the month's end.

I think a charge card is the way to go because you aren't building up a pile of debt and paying interest on it. But most of us wouldn't be able to afford to pay off our full card balance each month, so a credit card would be more reasonable, allowing you to make monthly payments toward your balance. It also helps you establish a credit history, which is key to being approved for a house, a car or any major purchase.

But if you can't afford to pay off your credit card within 3-6 months, you can't afford to use credit. Don't charge anything unless you can afford to pay more than the minimum payment or you won't pay off your balance until you have grand kids, more than 20 years from now. Seriously, I read a study that reported that if you make only the minimum monthly payment on your credit cards, it could take as many as 23 years to pay off each card. That's a long time, and it will cut into your retirement.

If you're a full-time student in college, you may start getting a bunch of credit card offers in the mail, but handpick the ones you want to accept because you don't want to be tempted to use all of that credit. After all, it's not free money. You have to pay it back with interest. So when choosing a credit card, you should compare the interest rate and the annual fee. You only need 3-5 credit lines to build a good credit history. I recommend starting off with just three because you can lose track of your purchases and if you have too many credit lines someone close to you can use one of your cards without your knowledge.

Beware of companies that send you cards with processing fees. Usually they start you off with a $300 credit limit and load you up with $150 in fees to set up the account, plus you have a high interest rate to pay back. If you don't pay off the balance by the due date, the card company will tack interest on your balance. And then, one shopping trip can put you over the card limit, which leads to an over-the-limit fee. Before you know it, you owe $400 on a card with a $300 credit limit and the balance keeps rising despite the fact that you make your minimum payments, probably $15, on time every month. I went through this a couple times before I learned my lesson. I hope you heed my warning now, so you won't have to go through that costly lesson.

Credit cards aren't all bad. You can use them to pay for vacation expenses if you don't want to carry around cash or traveler's checks. By doing so, your card company may reward you with points that can lead to discounts at restaurants, on airfare and various forms of entertainment. But make sure you can pay off your cards' balances within 30 days or a couple months to avoid paying a lot of interest charges. A charge card may be a better option for travel expenses because you pay back the entire balance at the end of the month and avoid interest fees.

Credit card companies make their money from charging you interest when you don't pay off your full balance each month and when you only make the minimum payment. Credit card companies don't expect you to pay off your full balance by the end of the month, so they look forward to charging you an interest rate that will be included in your minimum monthly payment, which is at least 1% of your balance. You should never make just the minimum payment on your monthly bill because interest will be added onto your balance each month, and as I mentioned earlier, it will take a long time to pay off the balance, possibly more than 20 years.

A law was recently passed that requires creditors to show on your monthly statement how long it will take you to pay off your balance if you only make the minimum payment. If you don't want to take 20 years to pay off each of your cards, don't make just the minimum payment and try to pay off your card in full within 3-6 months.

If you carry a balance on your cards, you should always pay your monthly bills within 10 days of the due date to avoid late fees and bad marks on your credit. When you pay 30 or more days after the due date, your late payment is reported to the three major credit agencies and your FICO credit score drops. Your FICO score is a rating given to you by each credit agency, Experian, Equifax and Transunion, and it determines your creditworthiness. You need a good FICO score, 640 and above, in order to be approved for a home or car loan and to be awarded a low interest rate, which means less money you owe back.

Never charge up to your credit limit or you can end up exceeding your balance and be charged a penalty. A good rule is to never charge more than 50% of your credit line. Creditors prefer that you keep your balance at 20-50% of your limit. If you make on-time payments for 3-6 months, you should be successful at requesting an increase to your credit limit.

More importantly, if you keep your balance low and make your monthly payments by the due date, your FICO credit score will climb and it could lead to amazing 0% interest credit offers.

Zero percent interest means you're borrowing money at no extra cost to you.

But beware of no interest credit offers. If you miss a payment or you're late making a payment, the 0% agreement will likely be negated and you will have to start paying interest on your loan.

However, 0% interest cards are good if you can pay off the balance before the promotion period ends, usually in three months to a year. For instance, you may be able to buy a $1,000 60-inch flat screen TV with no payments and no interest for three months and you can buy a new couch with no payments and no interest for an entire year. Just make sure you pay the account off before the promotion ends to avoid a huge interest rate. A high interest rate is good when you're saving your money, but it's bad when you're paying money back because it costs you more money.

When I graduated college, I completely furnished my apartment with a loan that required no payments and no interest for a year. I foolishly did not make one payment for the entire year. That's what the furniture company is betting so they make even more money off you with the interest charges. So after a year of making no payments on my new furniture, the furniture company charged interest on the full $1,500 balance and only required me to make minimum $15 monthly payments. I made the minimum payments and my balance climbed to $2,000 as interest kept adding up. Eventually, the balance ballooned to $3,800, more than double the cost of the furniture. So be careful with the 0% interest promotions.

You've probably noticed car dealers advertising 0% interest on a new car. That's a great way to buy a car because you are only financing your negotiated price and you won't have to pay any interest. But again, if you are late making a payment or you miss a payment, your creditor will likely start charging you interest for your new car and that could mean paying an extra $5,000 or double the negotiated price by the time you finish paying off your car.

For instance, when I had bad credit, I bought a car for $17,995 and I ended up paying $36,000 for the car after making all of the payments because of a 15% interest rate. With a 0% interest rate, I would have only paid the negotiated price for my car, plus taxes, tag and title and I would have saved at least $15,000 in interest, also known as finance charges.

So if you are offered 0% interest, you should jump on it. But only if you are sure you can afford to make your payments on time, and if you can pay off the balance before the end of the promotion period to avoid higher interest rates and paying double what your merchandise is worth.

And remember, if you carry a balance on your credit cards, always pay more than the minimum monthly payment to limit the amount you have to pay back.

Credit Card No-Nos

- *Don't use a credit card if you don't have a 6-12 month rainy day fund*
- *Don't charge up to the credit limit*
- *Don't carry a balance over 50%*
- *Don't pay just the minimum monthly payment*
- *Don't make your payments late by 30 days or more*
- *Don't carry a balance more than 3-6 months*

Quiz 9

Choose the best answer

1) It's best to pay your credit card bills within _________ days of the due date.
   A. 10 days
   B. 30 days
   C. 60 days

2) You should never make the _________ monthly payment on your credit cards.
   A. maximum
   B. minimum
   C. ultimate

3) Zero percent interest financing can cost you more money if you __________.

   A. pay your balance in full during the promotional period
   B. make your monthly payments on time
   C. skip payments, make late payments or no payments

Be Familiar With Your Credit Report

If you want to live in a swank place and drive a nice car, you should pay attention to your credit report.

You need good credit to finance a house and a nice car. And nowadays, your credit may determine whether you're hired for a job.

So you should be aware of what's on your credit report.

A credit report lists your home address, the last few places you've worked and all of the companies you owe money to or have paid back. It also shows whether you pay on time or late.

Three credit agencies update your credit report. They are Equifax, Transunion and Experian. These three agencies each assign you a Fair Isaac Corporation (FICO) score that rates how good you are at paying back what you owe. You can get a free annual credit report at www.annualcreditreport.com. But I subscribe to a monthly credit monitoring service to get fraud alerts in order to prevent identity theft and to monitor my credit as I pay off debt.

Your credit report will show you credit scores ranging from 300-900. Banks and other creditors use these scores to decide who to approve for credit cards and loans and how much interest to charge.

Your FICO credit score should at least be a 640 to be considered for a loan but shoot for at least the 700s, so you are entitled to the lowest interest rates for loans. A low interest rate means less money for you to pay back.

If you have a score below 600, you probably won't even be able to open a bank account and it may affect you being hired for a new job. And if you try to purchase a car, you will likely be charged a high interest rate, which can force you to pay back an extra $10,000-$15,000 by the time you finish paying off the $20,000 car loan.

But if you establish good credit and practice good spending habits, your bank and other banks will fall over themselves sending you extremely low interest rate loan offers in the mail to purchase a new car or to spend as you wish. But only accept their offers if you have a need and you can comfortably pay back the loan. Seek out those zero percent interest rates, but keep in mind that banks usually have a loop hole, that your interest rate can be raised tremendously if you make a late payment.

Banks and other creditors want to see that you can pay back what you owe by the payment due date. They want you to owe no more than 50% of your card limit, preferably 20%. So if you have a $1,000 credit line, you should not spend more than $200-$500.

Creditors don't want to see any collection accounts from companies you never paid back, and they don't want to see a lot of inquiries into your credit. So you shouldn't be filling out credit card applications at stores and mall/airport kiosks to receive free gifts because it adds inquiries to your credit report that bring down your credit score. Those stuffed animals and key chains are not worth lowering your credit score, which leads to a higher interest rate on future credit offers.

Although you're entitled to a free credit report each year, I would recommend getting a monthly subscription to a credit monitoring web site. It gives you daily access to what's on your credit report and you can see your credit scores rise or fall as you use credit. You should know your credit score before walking into a car dealership or applying for any loan. Knowledge truly is power because if you know you have a very good FICO score, you can negotiate a better interest rate for your loan. But it's best to get pre-approved for a loan at your bank to have even more negotiating power.

I have been a subscriber of a monthly credit monitoring service for years, and I have been able to log on any day to see bad debt fall off my credit as I pay it off. My credit score has climbed from the high 400s to the 700s.

A score above 700 is considered excellent credit, and you will be able to get a loan for anything you want, if your income allows. However your excellent credit rating makes you a target for identity theft, which is when someone steals your personal information to open up credit in your name and to charge expensive items that end up being on your credit report and it takes a lot of legal wrangling to clear your name, if at all.

You can head off identity theft by keeping a regular track of your credit report. You can do this by subscribing to a monthly service or by requesting your free annual credit report.

Monitor and use your credit wisely, so when it comes time to buy a home or a nice car, you won't have to feel as embarrassed as I used to feel when I needed my grandfather to co-sign for me to finance a car because of my poor credit. My poor credit led to me being charged a high interest rate that doubled the cost of my car over the life of the loan. Although I grossly overpaid for a car, I gladly paid my obligation because I value having good credit.

Don't ever consider ignoring your debt. Items can remain on your credit for seven years keeping you from buying a home, getting a low interest rate on a new car or being approved for a business loan.

Ignoring what you owe is a big mistake because collection agencies will tack their fees onto your unpaid balance and hound you with daily phone calls. Besides, your unpaid balances go on your credit report and ruin your chances of getting a loan when you really need it, such as for your first house or a new business venture.

So do your best to establish and maintain good credit.

If you don't have any credit, you need to establish a history. If you save for an emergency fund as I've recommended, your bank or credit union will have no problem approving you for a credit card. In fact, your bank will likely reach out to you first because you have shown the ability to save money.

If your bank won't approve you for a card because of your lack of a credit history, you can definitely be approved for a secured credit card. Basically, your bank or credit union would issue you a secured credit card based on how much money you reserve for the card. So for a $300 credit line on a secured card, you would allocate $300 from your savings. You would use the card like a regular credit card, not charging more than 50% of the $300, making your payments on time and making more than the minimum monthly payment. All along your bank would report your progress to the three credit bureaus to establish your credit history. If you're using your secured credit card responsibly, I'm sure your bank or credit union will offer you a regular credit card and you can close your secured card account once you pay off that balance and move the $300 back to your savings account.

Another simple way to establish credit is by opening a furniture account. But don't try to furnish an entire room. Buy a computer desk or a TV stand and pay it off. Then, open an account at an electronics store and buy a small TV or an inexpensive laptop and pay the item off. But do not close the furniture and electronics store accounts because your zero balances compared to your credit limit looks good to creditors and will boost your credit score.

I used this strategy when I was trying to build my first house to boost my credit from the high 400s to the mid-700s. To raise my credit score, I opened two store cards, was approved for two bank credit cards and I opened a furniture account. I kept a low balance on all my cards and paid off a computer desk from the furniture store within three months. I also paid off some bad debts that were in collection and had them removed from my credit. Plus, I had old debt that was more than seven years delinquent removed by law. All the while, I observed my progress and watched my three credit scores rise by logging in to the credit monitoring service I subscribed to.

Quiz 10

Choose the best answer

1) Which of the following is not a credit reporting agency?

   ____

   A. Express
   B. Experian
   C. Equifax

2) An excellent credit score is a __________.
   A. 750
   B. 550
   C. 350

3) To build a good credit rating, you should spend _________ of your credit limit.

   A. 20%

   B. 60%

   C. 100%

Plan For Retirement

Finally, we are at the chapter that I feel is the most important lesson that I can teach you.

Start saving for retirement now because the more time you have before retirement, the more time you have for your savings and investments to double, triple, quadruple and some.

But more importantly, you are making sure you are financially secure and don't have to be a statistic. A recent study found that 63 out of every 100 retirees over the age of 65 are dependent on someone else to survive. Only 1% is wealthy and only 4% are financially secure. This mirrors the current overall state of the U.S. economy, where 1% of the entire population controls most of the country's wealth.

I'm sure you've heard that Social Security may be bankrupt by the time you and I retire. Social Security taxes are taken from your paycheck and set aside for you to receive a monthly income check when you're a senior citizen. But because it is expected to be bankrupt by the time you need it, you may have to rely on your savings to take care of you in your old age.

The future of Social Security is so unsecure that last summer the administration decided to save $30-$60 million by no longer mailing out the individual annual statements that show your yearly taxable income and your projected monthly payout from Social Security when you retire at age 62 or older. It also shows your possible income if you were to become disabled and could no longer work. Since 1995, the SSA statement arrived in your mail three months before your birthday each year.

Workers who are 60 and older will still receive an annual statement in the mail, but younger workers will have to view their statements online at www.ssa.gov. In the last statement I received in the mail in 2010, I recall reading that my benefits could be cut by a third when I retire in more than 30 years because of the fragile state of the SSA trust fund.

In light of recent changes and the uncertainty of Social Security, you would be wise to plan for retirement as if you won't receive a monthly Social Security check. Then if Social Security is still around when you retire, your monthly Social Security check would be a bonus to what you have personally saved for retirement. In my line of work as an insurance agent, I meet with retirees daily who only receive $400-$1,400 per month on their Social Security check. Some of them supplement their income with a small pension from their job that brings them an extra $200-$1,200 per month. But how many jobs offer pensions nowadays? Very few. So you should contribute to your job 401K and save using other retirement vehicles.

You don't want to be in the predicament of the hundreds of seniors that I've met within the last five years. Most of them are struggling to get by on a Social Security check that is less than $1,500 per month. The overwhelming majority have less than $5,000 saved in the bank, usually about $100-$200.

So don't procrastinate. Start saving for your retirement sooner rather than later.

However, don't contribute to your job's 401K until you have saved for your rainy day fund because if an emergency hits, you don't want to be subject to taxes and early withdrawal penalties by taking money from your 401K prior to age 59 1/2.

Once you have stocked your emergency fund, then you should participate in your job's 401K program because you're not going to get a better return on your money. For instance, if your job is adding 50 cents to each of your dollars, that's a 50% return on your money. There's no other investment that can get you that kind of return consistently without risking your money in the stock market. However, you should only contribute up to your employer's match. So if your job matches up to 6% of your income, you should only contribute 6% of your income to your 401K. Remember your budget calls for saving 20% of your income, so put the other 14% in a combination of savings accounts, CDs, IRAs and other financial products that enable your money to grow. A personal banker or a financial advisor can help you figure out the right mix for your financial goals, but get recommendations on trusted professionals from family and friends.

Think long and hard before you open an IRA (Individual Retirement Account) because like a 401K, you may be penalized if you need the money earlier in life. Then, you need to understand there are two types of IRAs: a traditional and a Roth. As long as you don't touch the money early, a traditional IRA isn't taxed until you withdraw it during retirement and you will be forced to withdraw a portion of the money every year when you hit age 70 1/2. Before retirement, you can withdraw funds in your 401K and a traditional IRA for a short-term loan and you won't be taxed or penalized if you repay the money within 60 days. If you don't repay the loan by the deadline, the IRS will tax you and access a 10% early withdrawal penalty.

If you want more lenient access to your retirement contributions, you should lean toward a Roth IRA. You use after-tax dollars to fund a Roth, so you can withdraw your contributions at any time free of taxes and early withdrawal penalties and you won't have to repay the money. But you can't touch the interest your Roth earns or that will be taxed and you will be slapped with the early withdrawal penalty. When you retire, you can withdraw all of the money, including the interest, without being taxed like you would be with a traditional IRA. You also won't be forced to make withdrawals from your Roth at age 70 ½ if you don't want to.

However, an IRA may not be an option if you make a high six-figure income. Additionally, you can't put more than $5,000 per person, per year into an IRA, unless you are age 50 or older. So what if you want to contribute more?

Universal Life Insurance is a better option because you can sock away as much as you want each year and you have tax-free, penalty-free access to your money before age 59 ½ because you're using after-tax dollars to fund it. A UL also kills two birds with one stone by providing you with necessary life insurance and growing cash value at a very competitive interest rate.

A personal banker or a financial advisor would be able to assist you with funding an IRA, life insurance and several other investments to help you reach your retirement goals. They also can show you how your contributions can grow up until your retirement age. I recommend a professional who has a life insurance license and who has experience helping people prepare for retirement. An experienced life insurance professional can show you non-risky ways to grow your money for retirement.

You really don't need to put your money in the stock market to build a comfortable nest egg, but a personal banker or a financial advisor with a Series 6 or a Series 7 can advise you on mutual funds, bonds and stocks along with the risks and rewards of investing in the stock market.

But keep in mind that when the Great Recession hit the U.S. in 2008, many people lost lots of money in the stock market and were forced to postpone their planned retirement. So personally, I lean toward financial advisors who are also life insurance agents because they can put your money in less risky investments and they can show you how to protect your income from death, disability and lawsuits.

If you're in school or just graduated, you probably think you're too young to think about retirement, but believe me, your parents wish they started saving at your age. When I was a 20-year-old intern at a Memphis newspaper, I asked the business editor for financial advice, and he said he wished he had started thinking about investing when he was my age.

Let me give you an example of why time means money for you when saving and investing for retirement.

Let's say at age 24, you've saved for your 6-12 month rainy day fund, and you are ready to start saving for retirement. Using the rule of 72, you can have nearly $500,000 by the time you retire. The rule calls for dividing the average interest rate of your retirement account into 72 to determine how many years it takes for your money to double. So if your average interest rate is 6%, your money would double every 12 years.

So if at age 24 you are earning $25,000 a year and your employer has agreed to match your 401K contributions up to 6%, you should contribute 6% of your income ($1,500) into your job's 401K, and your employer would match 50 cents for each dollar ($750). The average yearly tax refund check is $3,000. If you deposit $2,000 of it into a Roth IRA each year and you take into account your 401K contributions and employer match, you are putting $4,250 per year toward your retirement.

That's nearly 20% of your $25,000 income, which is right in line with my 60-20-10-10 rule©. And you should have at least $800 of your income remaining every year to put into savings accounts, plus $1,000 leftover from your annual tax refund check to save for your other financial goals, such as a down payment for a house, going on a trip around the world or whatever your dreams are. Also based on my rule, you would have ample money for living expenses.

If for the next 12 years, you contribute to your 401K and save part of your tax refund checks annually into a Roth IRA while averaging a modest 6% interest, you would have at least $60,000 by age 36. If you never save another dollar for retirement, based on the rule of 72 at 6% interest, your money would double every 12 years. So it would double 3x by the time you retire at age 72. Here's an example of how your money can double every 12 years using the rule of 72 with a 6% interest rate:

Age 36: $60,000

Age 48: $120,000

Age 60: $240,000

Age 72: $480,000

That's nearly $500,000 after only saving toward retirement for 12 years. If you continue to save for most of your working years, you should have at least $1 million when you retire. If you retire with $1 million, you can have a personal banker or a financial advisor place your money into a deferred annuity that could generate a $50,000 yearly income for life based on a 5% payout factor. If you stopped your retirement savings early and only have $500,000, you could earn $25,000 annually in a deferred annuity based on a 5% payout factor. However you never should put all of your eggs into one basket, so spread your money around into several annuities with different insurance companies. You still would be able to generate the annual income I mentioned previously, it would just come to you separately from your various annuities.

By the time you retire, your house should be paid off, but if you need more money than your investments offer, you still would have access to your balance. However, you wouldn't need to touch your balance if you've been saving in other accounts through the years. If so, you also would have tens of thousands or more in savings and CDs. And you may even receive Social Security payouts.

So your retirement would be far more financially secure than most seniors, including the ones I've met over the years who struggle on $18,000 or less per year.

Hence, start talking to a personal banker or financial advisor now to begin planning for your retirement and don't set yourself back by touching your 401K or IRA funds until you quit working for good to avoid paying income taxes and an additional 10% early withdrawal penalty for taking the money before age 59 ½. So if you switch jobs, don't spend the money in your 401k. Roll it over into an IRA or your next job's 401k, if that's an option.

When I left my last newspaper job, I withdrew the $3,000 from my 401K instead of rolling the money into my next job's 401K or an IRA. I was hit with $800 in income taxes and an early withdrawal penalty during tax season. That was the first year that I did not receive a tax refund check. Instead, I owed the government $1,000.

You won't have to touch your 401k or your IRA because of a job loss or some other financial emergency if you continually build up your rainy day fund and other savings accounts by always saving part of your income each month.

So if you save regularly and invest in your 401K and a Roth IRA, you won't have to worry about the uncertainty of Social Security and you certainly won't have to greet people at Wal-Mart to make ends meet when you retire. Instead, you will be able to relax with a comfortable nest egg and side dishes of savings accounts and CDs while sipping pina coladas on a beach, a cruise ship or wherever you wish to spend your time to reflect on the amazing life you will have created by using the financial principles I have taught you in this book.

The Rule of 72

Financial advisors use the rule of 72 to determine how many years it takes for your money to double before your retirement by dividing your average interest rate on your investments into 72. Here's an example:

If you have contributed $60,000 into a Roth IRA by age 36 and the average interest rate is 6%, you divide 6 into 72 and discover that your money doubles every 12 years. So if you plan to retire at age 72, your money would double 3x by then to $480,000.

Age 36: $60,000

Age 48: $120,000

Age 60: $240,000

Age 72: $480,000

Quiz 11

Choose the best answer

1) An IRA is the/an _________.
   A. Internal Revenue Association
   B. Internet Reporting Agency
   C. Individual Retirement Account

2) The rule of _________ is a formula that shows how many years it takes for your money to double.
   A. 24
   B. 72
   C. 98

3) The penalty for an early 401K or IRA withdrawal is _________.
   A. 10%
   B. 25%
   C. 50%

Quiz Answers

Quiz 1: B, C, C

Quiz 2: True, False, True

Quiz 3: B, B, B

Quiz 4: True, False, True

Quiz 5: B, A, B

Quiz 6: True, False, False

Quiz 7: B, B, B

Quiz 8: False, False, True

Quiz 9: A, B, C

Quiz 10: A, A, A

Quiz 11: C, B, A

Making More Sense Out Of Your Dollars

Make a habit of giving

You know there are a lot of homeless people walking around who could use your designer loafers and name brand sneakers that collect dust in your closet because you think they're out of style. Get a box and gather up all of your old clothes and shoes and take them to the nearest Salvation Army or Goodwill. Figure out the cash value of your charity items and you can deduct it on your taxes.

Give a consistent offering to your church. Church leaders like to preach for you to give 10% of your gross income, but give whatever you can afford.

Give money to a friend in need without expecting the person to repay you, but only give what you can afford to not have repaid.

Treat your parents to dinner or a movie to show your gratitude for bringing you into this world.

When you do nice things for other people, good things will come back to you, and giving makes you feel good inside.

Do not loan money. Instead give it away.

I'm sure you've heard the passage from the Bible that says, 'Neither a borrower nor a debtor be." Don't fall into the habit of loaning money to people or owing people money.

Loaning and borrowing money can ruin your friendships and family relations when the money isn't paid back.

I know I said you should give. But there is a difference between giving and loaning. When you give money, you don't expect it back. When you loan or borrow money, it is expected to be paid back and it often is not. So don't loan money if you can't afford to lose it forever.

Be smart about college spending and avoid student loans

If you're just out of high school, I recommend staying close to home for college if your parents can't foot the bill without taking equity out of their house. If you stay home for college, you don't have to worry about room and board and can just apply for government grants to pay for tuition and books and you would likely have money remaining for discretionary spending and saving. Going out of state is a luxury you can't afford because out-of-state tuition is more than 2x the cost of in-state tuition, plus you'd have to pay for rent, groceries, utilities and other living expenses. But if you really feel compelled to leave your home state, establish residency in the state where you want to attend college by living there for six months in order to be eligible for in-state tuition.

Do your best to avoid student loans because it's the only debt that can't be wiped off your credit during bankruptcy. It can be very tempting to take out a student loan to afford to pay your rent, to go shopping and pay for trips, but you will feel the repercussions for decades to come.

I have a family member who owes $100,000 in student loans and said it's unlikely the debt will be paid off this lifetime. Unpaid student loans follow you to your grave. Recently, a Washington Post article revealed that Americans owe more than $800 billion in student loans, surpassing credit card debt and auto loans. The article also reported that senior citizens owe $36 billion in student loans and some are getting their Social Security checks garnished to repay what they owe from attending college decades ago. In the article, the president of a consumer bankruptcy association said student loans are like a ball and chain that you drag through life and you can finally unhook the chain when you get into a coffin. President Obama is addressing the issue by signing off on a program that forgives federal student loans after an individual has paid 10% of his or her income toward paying back the loans for 20 years.

You don't have to get student loans, at least as an undergraduate, pursuing an associate or bachelor's degree. I earned my four-year degree without taking out a student loan or my mother paying any of my tuition. So far my oldest son is attending college for free. He gets enough federal and state grants to pay for his tuition and books, and he has money left over to take care of his living expenses for months. He also gets paid by his college to be a student ambassador and to manage the newsletter for students.

When I pursued my associate of arts degree and my bachelor's in journalism, I received federal and state grants and I won a couple of journalism scholarships. My grades were a mixture of As, Bs and Cs and only 3 Ds – pardon the pun -- throughout high school and college.

The key to making decent grades is just completing all of your class assignments, participating in class discussions, taking notes in class and studying your notes to pass your exams. Instructors just want to see you make a good effort.

By doing so, you would be averaging at least a B in your cumulative classes, which is good enough to receive an academic grant and to qualify for scholarships. However, you don't have to possess an above average grade point average to receive free money for college. Just complete a financial assistance application at www.fafsa.gov and more than likely you will receive some money, but it will be passed to you through the college you chose. You may want your parent or guardian to help you complete the application.

You also don't have to be a straight A student to earn college scholarships although it helps. But you can use your natural talents, such as art, writing, and sports, to earn scholarships. You also can earn scholarships through connections you make by being involved in school clubs and your church. It pays to be active. I was awarded two of my college scholarships because I hung out around the internship, scholarship and employment office for my major.

Do whatever you have to that's legal, but don't get student loans for college.

Don't be in a hurry to move out on your own

I know young people want freedom away from parents and guardians. I couldn't wait to move out of my mother's house. But if I could do it all over again, I would have made the most out of living at home instead of being in a rush to get my own place. My mother told me to move back home to save money, but I moved back home for just a few months and I didn't save any money. In fact, I spent most of my money and went to cash advance stores and pawned my stuff to help pay my bills.

I don't want young people to make the same mistake. Make the most out of living at home once you become an adult, so you will be financially secure and prepared for whenever you or your parents decide it's time for you to move out on your own.

I recommend moving back home after college and using your time at home to pay off any credit cards or student loans you decided to get against my advice. Also, find out how much it would cost to rent your own place and for electricity and cable. Then, figure up a budget based on my 60-20-10-10 rule© and begin saving for your emergency fund if you haven't already. It should take you no more than five years to get your finances in order if you move back with your family after college. If you don't go off to college, it should only take you three years to get your finances in order. Once you are debt free and have saved your 6-12 month rainy day fund, you are financially secure enough to get your own place, unless you just want to stay home by choice.

Make sure you have health and life insurance

Like a car, your body is going to need a regular checkup to make sure everything is working properly. And if you neglect these checkups, you can end up in the emergency room trying to get down to the bottom of your pain.

If you have health insurance, you are more likely to make regular visits to a doctor to make sure you are functioning OK.

If you're younger than age 26, you can stay on your parents' health insurance policy. And many colleges have student health plans. Then, when you're in your career, make sure to sign up for your company's health plan.

Also, make sure you or your parents have a $10,000-$20,000 life insurance policy on you because millions of young people are dying every year from car accidents and sudden deaths and you don't want your family to be burdened with the costs of your burial while they're already grieving your loss.

If someone depends on your income, talk to a personal banker or a financial advisor about obtaining the proper amount of life insurance for your loved ones to maintain their lifestyle if you die prematurely. So if you make $30,000 per year and you are married or you have dependents, you should have 10-25 times your annual salary, which would be $300,000-$750,000. Again, a financial advisor or personal banker, who is licensed to sell life insurance, can guide you.

Don't have a wedding on credit

Arguing about money is the No. 1 cause of divorce for young couples. So if you choose to marry, don't start your new life together with the financial strain of paying off a credit card bill from a half-day wedding and celebration.

Have a small gathering at your church or get married at the courthouse. Then, splurge on a nice honeymoon and host a small reception at the home you are able to buy and decorate nicely with the money you saved by skipping the big wedding.

As I write this, a guy called into a financial advice show, about being stressed that he's unable to help his fiancé pay for their wedding because he has $70,000 in student loan debt. The wedding costs $40,000, and the guy couldn't understand that he and his bride-to-be should use the money to put a down payment on a house or to pay down his student loans. He was only concerned about their families wanting wedding memories. But nowadays, the average U.S. marriage lasts for eight years.

So, skip the big wedding. Have a small reception with family and friends. And if you happen to still be married in 10 years, have a big wedding vow renewal ceremony, but not on credit.

Decide the right time to buy a home

Buying a home is considered to be the leading source of wealth in the United States. Unlike rent, every monthly mortgage payment goes toward equity – the amount your house is worth versus how much you owe -- in your home. The equity could be used to pay off student loans, to fund a dream vacation or to start a new business.

If you don't want the responsibility of mowing the lawn and other landscaping, you should buy a condo or a townhome. A condo looks like an apartment, but you own your unit, and association fees pay for the upkeep of the community's common areas. A townhome looks like a two-story house and has a yard, but it is connected to other townhomes in a row. The newer townhome communities maintain the surroundings through association fees.

You can't go wrong choosing a townhome, a condo or a single-family home, which is a stand-alone house. It's better to finance a home that goes toward building equity than throwing away tens of thousands into renting and being subjected to yearly rent increases. If your rent is $600 per month, you are throwing away $7,200 per year. That's $72,000 in 10 years. Before I bought my house, my rent averaged $1,000 per month, which is $12,000 per year and I rented for 11 years, so I threw away almost $150,000 that could have been used toward home ownership.

However, you should rent if you're unsure on whether you want to stay in your current town for at least four years. If you finance a residence and need to move in a few years to accept a job promotion elsewhere, you will have the burden of trying to sell your home and you likely won't get a fair return on your investment.

You also should continue to rent rather than purchase a home if you don't have your 6-12 month rainy day fund in addition to a down payment because if something breaks down or needs to be upgraded, you will have to shoulder the bill unlike renting a place when you can just call the landlord or property manager to fix the problem.

Letter From The Author

Well, I hope you have found my book to be enlightening. I threw a lot of information at you that I hope you use to avoid making the financial mistakes that I once made.

Let's recap the points I made:

1) Work at something you enjoy
2) Don't spend your whole paycheck
3) How much you make doesn't matter
4) Live on a budget based on my 60-20-10-10 rule©
5) Save for a rainy day
6) Treat yourself
7) Use a checking account responsibly
8) Be careful with credit
9) Be familiar with your credit report
10) Plan for retirement

If you incorporate my advice into your life, you won't have to stress about money and you will enjoy financial security to enjoy life and to live comfortably. I don't expect you to pick up these lessons right away, so I recommend you read this book a couple more times. You also should subscribe to my YouTube videos, free of charge, at www.youtube.com/teneshialafaye and visit my blog, www.mytensense.com, to stay current on my financial advice. For regular updates of my blog and videos, follow me on Twitter, www.twitter.com/teneshialafaye and like my Facebook page, http://www.facebook.com/MyTenSense.

If you have any questions about your personal financial situation, send me an email at teneshia@mytensense.com or a personal message on Facebook or Twitter. I wish you lots of financial peace and happiness.

Take care,

Teneshia LaFaye

Made in the USA
Monee, IL
04 November 2026

67380513R00049